15 Minutes

INCLUDING

Q&A

A PLAN TO SAVE THE WORLD
FROM LOUSY PRESENTATIONS

JOEY ASHER

Persuasive
Speaker
Press

atlanta, georgia

For Spring Asher,

my mom, who taught me the value of keeping it simple.

CONTENTS

INTRODUCTION

ALL PRESENTATIONS SHOULD BE LIMITED TO 15 MINUTES INCLUDING Q&A

Most business presentations stink. Really stink. They stink in a way that drains souls. They stink in a way that makes people think to themselves, "I flew in from L.A. for this? Maybe my mom was right. Maybe I should have gone to medical school."

Exactly how do presentations stink?

They ramble on.

They fail to make any points.

They try to say so many things that they become unwieldy PowerPoint Death Stars with no impact.

They ignore key audience concerns.

They fail to tell a simple story that takes the listener on a journey.

They're delivered with all the energy of one of those ferns that adorn the reception areas of every corporate office on the planet.

They almost never include anything fun and animating, like stories, anecdotes, or analogies.

They don't leave enough time for questions.

What's the result of these terrible presentations?

We waste time: time that could be spent with clients or prospects, time that could be spent training personnel, time that could be spent executing the dozens of things that need to be done to make money.

This book lays out a plan to fix all that.

Here's the plan:

From now on, all presentations should be no longer than 15 minutes. Half of that time is for the prepared message. The rest is for Q&A.

Step 1. Prepare a Seven-Minute Rifle Shot Presentation

When I tell people that they should never prepare more than seven minutes of formal presentation, some look at me like I've been smoking crack. Seven minutes? It takes most people seven minutes just to give the background on their research. "Before we get started, let me detail our methodology." To which I say, "Who cares about your freakin' methodology? Is it going to make my job easier?" I doubt it.

Seven minutes seems too short because almost no one in business knows how to craft a message in a simple straight line. But my company has worked with thousands of business people across all industries. And we have found that if you're focused, you can usually say everything you need to say in seven minutes. This book will lay out a simple approach for doing just that.

Step 2. Allow Listeners to Fill in the Blanks and Raise Objections With Q&A

Q&A is the magic that makes this plan work. Q&A ensures that you cover everything important to the audience. After all, by leaving half of your time for Q&A, the audience gets to ask all the questions it wants. "You didn't touch on the cost of adding all of these new projects. Can you address that?" Your answer: "Absolutely, the cost will be…"

Q&A also adds persuasive magic. It allows you to address the audience's objections. "Don't you think that you're underestimating the number of clients that will abandon us during the next quarter with your plan?" Your answer: "I certainly can understand why you would feel that way. But let me say why I don't think we should be worried about that issue…"

Answer audience objections well and you'll win them over.

Step 3. Deliver the Presentation With Intensity

Most business people speak with all of the intensity of a houseplant. With that in mind, if you want to set yourself apart from the pack, then you need to speak with some passion. We recommend adopting the "intense dinner conversation style." In other words, speak to your audience like you're having a highly animated dinner conversation.

How you look and sound matters. If you want to be good at this, you're going to have work on your style.

Lemmings Don't Speak Well

If you're going to adopt the "15 Minutes Including Q&A" approach, you're going to have to dump some common corporate practices.

You can't create good presentations if the first thing you do is search for the slides you used on a "similar presentation" from last month. Even if someone told you the presentation was great—and

I'll bet my lungs it wasn't that great—it won't cut it. You need fresh thought for every presentation.

You can't give a good presentation if you insist on starting your presentation by saying, "First, let me start by giving you a little background." Of course, what you're really saying is, "I want to tell you everything I've done over the last several weeks, because I have no idea how to put all this information into some sort of comprehensible story."

If you insist on walking everyone through an entire spreadsheet that they could read on their own, you won't do well. More importantly, your audience will be bored.

If you insist on giving those "quarterly update" presentations where all you do is review everything that everyone already knows, then you're also in trouble. I spoke with a manager who gave one of those "update" presentations every quarter. She admitted to me that no one liked them or found them valuable. When I asked why she delivered them anyway she said, "Well, it's expected."

Lemmings don't become good public speakers.

"15 Minutes Including Q&A" Can Happen in Our Lifetime

I was doing a workshop recently for a huge international financial services company. During a break, I asked, "What would happen if the CEO decreed that from now on all presentations would last no longer than 15 minutes including Q&A?"

Several people said, "We couldn't do it."

"Why not?" I said.

"Because it's not our culture," went the argument. "We blow our nose and produce six slides. We can't be that short."

"But," I argued, "what if the CEO decreed it and made it law? What would happen?"

"At first, we would scream," one person said. "Then we would become efficient."

That's typical of the reaction I get any time I propose my 15-minutes-including-Q&A revolution. People say, "At first it would be hard. But eventually we'd love it."

Countless people are fed up with sitting through rotten, time-wasting presentations.

We can fix that problem by following the ideas in this book.

So read on, my fellow revolutionaries. You have nothing to lose but your PowerPoint templates.

PART I

PREPARE A SEVEN-MINUTE RIFLE SHOT PRESENTATION

1

A PLAN FOR A SEVEN-MINUTE PRESENTATION

How to Say a Lot in a Short Period of Time

For most people, requiring that they give their presentation in seven minutes or less will seem absurd. "How can I do that? I've spent a month on this project! Now you want me to say everything in seven minutes? Impossible!"

But it's not that hard if you keep a simple principle in mind. Your goal isn't to tell everything you did. It's to help your listeners with their lives.

If you think in terms of simply helping your listeners with their lives, then things get much simpler.

Start your presentation by putting your finger on the key issue or question that your audience cares about. Then detail how you plan to help them with that issue. Problem—Solution. Challenge—Response. Question—Answer.

To give your presentation in seven minutes, focus everything around this simple model. You don't have to worry about leaving things out because your audience will have plenty of time to ask questions.

Here's a plan that will allow you to say a lot in seven minutes or less:

STEP 1. THE HOOK—30 SECONDS

Start by putting your finger on the business issue that your audience cares most about. A good way to arrive at your hook is to think, "If I were to ask my audience what worried them most about the topic I'm going to talk to them about, what would they say?"

The hook often starts with the following phrase, "I understand that you are concerned about . . ."

STEP 2. THE PREVIEW—30 SECONDS

Give a quick overview that details how you plan to address the problem. The idea is to give your audience the three thoughts that they must remember above all else. Another way to think of this is "What are my three takeaway 'bumper stickers?'"

STEP 3. THE BODY OF THE PRESENTATION—FIVE MINUTES

Once you've come up with your three takeaway points, go into detail about each of the "bumper stickers."

The pattern to follow is to give a couple of sentences of explanation. Then give some evidence in support of your points. The evidence can be anecdotes, data, analogies, etc. Great speakers use lots of stories.

STEP 4. THE RECAP—30 SECONDS

This is where you remind the listeners of your three key points. Simply repeat your three key messages from the preview verbatim. Don't get fancy here. This part is simply about driving home the key points.

STEP 5. CALL TO ACTION—30 SECONDS

You always want to end by telling your audience the next step. It may be the next step for them. It may be the next step you will take. It may be the approval that you need from them to proceed. But you want to give a sense of direction. What's next?

KEY TAKEAWAY

You can say a lot in a short period of time, but only if you approach your presentation with focus. Start by shining a spotlight on the audience's key business issue. Then lay out in three steps your plan to help solve the problem.

2

WHAT A SEVEN-MINUTE PRESENTATION SOUNDS LIKE

Yes, You Really Can Say a Lot in Just Seven Minutes

S till not convinced that you can say much in seven minutes? Below is a presentation given by one of my clients (I've disguised the company to respect confidentiality). It was delivered by a division president of a manufacturing organization to his board of directors regarding his plans to guide the division back toward profitability. It took about seven minutes to deliver aloud. It says a lot because it follows a simple approach that focuses solely on the listeners' needs.

STEP 1. THE HOOK—INTRODUCE THE BUSINESS PROBLEM

"When you appointed me to lead this turnaround several months ago, production quality

was terrible. As a result our best customers were leaving us and our revenues were falling. You wanted me to bring the organization back to profitability by the fourth quarter of next year. That means we need to increase revenues by $8 million.

"I believe that goal is possible. I want to talk to you about how we'll reach it."

STEP 2. THE PREVIEW—GIVE A THREE-POINT OVERVIEW

"I have a three-step plan to reach our goal:

- *First, we need to continue the recruiting that has already started in order to turn around our quality.*
- *Second, we need to win back our old customers. That will get us $5 million in revenues.*
- *Third, we need to make up the rest with sales of new products."*

STEP 3. THE BODY OF THE PRESENTATION—
RESTATE EACH POINT. EXPLAIN EACH POINT.
GIVE EXAMPLES ILLUSTRATING EACH POINT.

"Let's start with the first point: **We need to continue the recruiting that has already started in order to turn around our quality.**

"When my predecessor left, we lost three of our four plant managers. We immediately started getting complaints from clients. At our Albany site, the packaging was poorly glued. At the St. Louis site, there were holes in the gloves. At the Minneapolis site, we could not meet client delivery deadlines.

"In every case, the problem wasn't the manufacturing process. Nothing was happening that couldn't be fixed quickly. The problem was communication between the plant managers and the customers. Jack Smith at Cralizon, our biggest customer for our glove products, told me that when he called about the glue problem six months ago, he left a voicemail and no one got back to him. He left a second voicemail and no one got back to him. When he got another ship-

14

ment with poorly glued boxes, he fired us and started getting his supply from our competition.

"We've had the same problem with other sites. We would have something go wrong, and while we certainly needed to look at what was going wrong with the process, the bigger problem was simply a communication breakdown.

"We've started to right the ship by hiring new plant managers for the Albany and Minneapolis plants. When we hired John Fredericks for the Albany plant, the first thing I told him was that I wanted him personally handling all customer complaints. I said the same thing to Alan Constantine at our Minneapolis plant. As a result, we seem to have the problems ironed out at those plants.

"We still haven't found anyone for the St. Louis plant. We have a headhunter who is working on that project but just haven't found the right person yet. In the meantime, I have appointed Alex Jacobs, the assistant plant manager, to oversee the plant. He's not right for the job. But I'm working with him until we find his replacement. We have some good candidates. I think we will have some good news in the next month.

"The bottom line is that we've made progress and we need to continue to hire to replenish lost talent.

"Let's move to the second point: **We need to win back our old customers. That will get us $5 million in revenues.**

"The good news is that none of our customers really wanted to leave us. They just got so fed up that they were forced to leave. We had served them well for years. And none have been happy working with our competition after leaving us. If we can convince them that we've fixed the quality problems, I'm confident they will return.

"I know this because I've spent the last three months personally calling on our biggest accounts. Six weeks ago, I sat in the office of John Castro of Cantor Williams Jones. I went to see him with the intent of letting him vent, telling me why he left us. He said, 'I can't stand the supplier we have right now. Our current supplier doesn't seem to be able to deliver on time. Ever. But it's a lesser of two evils thing. They're late, but your boxes were falling apart. Right now, we just have to make do with a poor situation.'

"When I asked him if he would give us another chance, he said he would consider placing a small order as a test. I then sent John Fredericks out to meet him and they've started to build a good relationship. I'm told that we're probably going to get that business back in six months. And I think we have similarly good stories with our other clients.

"The fact is that our clients loved us until we dropped the ball. They're willing to come back if we can show them we've made changes.

"My third key point is: **We need to make up the rest with sales of new products.**

"The visits to angry clients yielded some opportunities. We met last week with William First from Jackson Hole Rubber Products. He told me that he was interested in creating a thick rubber glove for the foot. You heard me right. He wants gloves for the foot.

"He wants to capitalize on the growing trend for minimalist running shoes. Turns out that there are a lot of people who want to run barefoot. But they can't run in the streets without cutting their feet. So they want to put a thick rubber glove on their feet that will allow them the feel of running barefoot.

"Given our existing technology, we can produce this product for them pretty quickly and easily. In fact, we already have a team at their site, putting together specs. We expect to have a prototype for them in a few weeks. They say that they will put in a $1 million order in six months.

"We have several other opportunities in the pipeline."

STEP 4. RECAP YOUR THREE KEY MESSAGES

"I'm confident that we're going to meet our goal of growing revenues by $8 million in 18 months.

"As I said, the key is three things:

- *Recruiting managers for key plant positions.*

- *Winning back our old customers.*
- *Growing revenues with new products."*

STEP 5. CALL TO ACTION

"I'd like your support as we move forward with this plan."

KEY TAKEAWAY

You can say a lot in a short period of time, but only if you approach your presentation with focus. Start by shining a spotlight on the audience's key business issue. Then lay out in three steps your plan to help solve the problem. Then bring to life each of the three points with a brief explanation followed by an example, anecdote, or other form of evidence.

Then recap and make a final call to action.

3

START BY FOCUSING ON THE KEY BUSINESS CHALLENGE

"What's the Best Way to Start My Presentation?"

Our presentation model is a simple story-telling model. We start with a challenge. Then we take the listener on a journey toward resolution.

Identify a challenge. Resolve it.

With that in mind, how do you start your presentation?

You hook your listener at the beginning by identifying a challenge he or she cares about. That grabs their attention because the promise is that you're going to resolve the challenge.

Consider *Jaws*. If you've seen the movie, you remember how it starts. The girl goes swimming and gets eaten by the shark.

First scene! Boom. We've got a shark eating swimmers. Now that's a problem! We're hooked. The rest of the movie is a resolution of the problem set up in that first scene. And when they kill the shark at the end, the story is finished. Problem–Resolution.

A great presentation does the same thing. In the first scene, describe the shark that's threatening the swimmers. Put another way, start your presentation by putting your finger on the audience's pressing issue. Then promise to help them with the issue.

Don't start by giving a bunch of background about your approach. Don't tell the history of your project. Don't do anything other than shine a light on the audience's key problem.

What if your audience is an organization that is charged with increasing revenues by $10 million in six months? Everyone in the audience is concerned about how to accomplish that feat. Your hook might sound like this:

> *"We're charged with increasing revenues by $10 million in six months. I'm going to talk about how we're going to do it."*

Or what if your audience is a group of bankers who are overwhelmed with the burden of complying with new regulations? Your hook might sound like this:

> *"The regulators have put in place a series of credit reporting obligations that are going to be extremely time consuming. I know that you're worried about adding headcount. We need a plan to ensure that we comply without having to add headcount. I'm going to talk about how we're going to do it."*

Or what if you have to speak to employees about a new system for logging travel expenses? Your hook might sound like this:

> *"We've just put in place a new process for logging travel expenses. Everyone here is going to have to use the new system. I know that you like the current system. But I also know that you would like to save time. Well, this new system can save you time. I'm going to talk about how to use the new system."*

Or what if you're trying to get employees at your company to come forward with patentable ideas? Your hook might sound like this:

> *"Everyone here is interested in earning more money in their paycheck. And you may not know it, but you may have a patentable idea that can help you earn more money. I'm going to talk to you today about how you can capture that idea and make more money."*

Or what if you're talking to a distribution partner who wants good products to sell to end users? Your hook might sound like this:

> *"I know that you're interested in growing your sales with your industrial clients. I'm going to talk to you about a new protective glove product that your prospects will love and that can grow your revenues."*

Ways to Jazz Up Your Hook

If you're putting your finger firmly on your listeners' needs, they'll pay attention. You don't need anything clever. But some people like to make their hooks "sexy." Here are some ideas.

You might want to tell a story.

> *"Last week, I went into one of our stores looking for a white t-shirt. They had none in my size. I found out that last year we lost $40 million because we were out of stock when customers came in for specific items. Out-of-stocks is a problem that we all recognize. I'm going to talk about how we can fix that problem."*

You might want to use a compelling piece of data.

> *"Imagine $10 million dollars a year. That's how much money we stand to save if we can eliminate the paper invoices that we create each year on our loading docks nationwide. I'd like to talk about a plan to capture those savings."*

What if You Don't Know Your Audience's Key Business Issue?

If you don't know the key driving need from your audience's perspective, your presentation is probably not going to be good. The only reason anyone listens to anything is to find solutions to problems they care about.

In workshops, clients often say that they sometimes don't know their audience's key challenges.

"If I'm going in to see the CFO, I often don't have a strong sense of his or her key issues."

I understand that finding out your audience's key issues can be difficult. But a strong understanding of your audience's issues is as important to your presentation as the foundation is to a house. You just can't do a good job without it.

So if you really want to do well, then find time to call up members of your audience and ask them what is important to them. Or send them an email with a question or two. Or at least find someone who is well-acquainted with the audience and ask them.

Otherwise, you're doomed and so is your audience.

KEY TAKEAWAY

To grab your listeners at the beginning of your presentation, describe the key business problem that your audience is most concerned about. Then promise to help them address that problem.

4

FOCUS YOUR PRESENTATION
ON THREE KEY MESSAGES

How to Simplify Any Message

Most presentations are undisciplined messes. They ramble on without making any discernible points. With the "15 Minutes Including Q&A" approach, you make three clear points. That's all.

"Can I make four points?"

Sure. But you won't be using this approach. And remember that it's a slippery slope. I've found that most people can decide on the three most important things to say.

Getting this right is perhaps the most challenging part of this approach. But it's the most critical.

Use the same approach that I used when my daughter Annie had to give a speech to the fifth grade class at Dunwoody Springs Middle School. Annie was running for class secretary. She had written out her speech on a sheet of notebook paper and showed it to me. When I proceeded to tear it apart (critically, not literally), she got mad at me and stormed out the door.

After I apologized, I said, "Annie, what are three things you really want them to remember about you? Tell me in three short sentences."

She thought about it for a moment and then said, "First, I will work hard. Second, I will be a good listener. Third, I will make sure that we keep the bathrooms clean."

Perfect!

That's the exact same approach that I've used with Presidents and CEOs of companies. The power question here is:

Assuming that your audience will forget most of what you will say, what are the three things that you absolutely want them to remember?

Here's another way that I ask the same question:

What are the three bumper sticker takeaways for this presentation?

By a "bumper sticker," I mean that the point should be no longer than six to eight words.

Shorter than that and you lose meaning. Longer than that and you lose your audience.

Here's a good bumper sticker: "We can save you money."

Here's another version of the same bumper sticker that's too short: "Money." It just doesn't say enough.

Here's another version of the same bumper sticker that's too long: "We can save you money by cutting down hospital stays, reducing ER visits, and cutting out waste fraud and abuse." Too much. Save the detail for the body of the presentation.

Examples of What Your Three Bumper Stickers Could Sound Like

From a health insurance executive's presentation on the value of managed care:

- We save money.
- We improve health care quality.
- We allow for greater coverage of underserved populations.

From a management consultant's proposal to revise a business process:

- Your automobile leasing process is costly.
- Automation should streamline the process.

- How we expect to save you $500,000 a year.

From a lobbyist seeking regulatory approval of a plan proposed by an electric utility:

- It's good for the ratepayers.
- It's good for the electric utility.
- It's good for the state.

From a lawyer's presentation on how to avoid anti-trust liability:

- Topics to avoid when talking to competitors.
- How to go about harming your competitor.
- Be careful what you put in documents.

Some Standard Approaches That Work For a Lot of Presentations

A standard past–present–future approach:

- In the past we've done this . . .
- Right now we're doing this . . .
- In the future, we will probably do this . . .

Weighing the pros and cons:

- The pros for this approach are . . .
- The cons for this approach are . . .
- My recommendation is . . .

Selling a new idea:

- The current situation is . . .
- The challenge we're facing is . . .
- The solution I recommend is . . .

KEY TAKEAWAY

Simplify your message by focusing on three messages. Ask yourself, "What are the three things I really want my audience to remember?" Then put those things into three "bumper stickers" for the audience to remember.

5

FILLING OUT YOUR THREE KEY MESSAGES

Address the Audience's Basic Questions About Each Point

Once you've decided on your three key points (or bumper stickers), the next step is to fill out those points. But you still need to keep it simple. Remember that you only have seven minutes. Total!

Each point can be no longer than two or three minutes. To keep each point tight, give a brief explanation. Give some evidence. Then stop.

Explain Your Point by Giving a Simple Answer to the Basic Questions

To bring to life each point, imagine a conversation with a key listener. What would that person ask you about each point? Answer those questions. Cite some evidence or examples in support of your answer. Then stop and move on to the next point.

EXAMPLE 1: MANAGED HEALTH CARE

Let's say that your presentation is about how managed health care is a good thing for the economy. One of your three bumper sticker points might be: "Managed health care saves money."

What is the first question that a key listener might ask? How about: "How does it save money?" If that's the key question, then the beginning of that point should be a couple of sentences answering that question.

> *"Let's talk about how managed health care saves money. Managed health care saves money in several ways. It saves money by shortening or eliminating hospital stays. It saves money by eliminating waste fraud and abuse. It saves money by incenting doctors to prescribe generic drugs as opposed to far more expensive non-generics."*

Next, you should cite evidence in support of your explanation.

Data Evidence: *"Patients on managed health care spent on average 50 percent less time in hospitals than those not on managed health care. That saves a lot of money. In fact, last year the average cost per hospital stay per patient was $10,000 for managed care as compared to $100,000 for those not on managed care."*

Story Evidence: *"It's amazing how easily managed health care can save money on prescription drugs. Here's how the drug system works. A drug rep visits a doctor and tells her all about the latest pain medication. The rep leaves samples and urges the doctor to let her patients try it out. So the next time a patient comes in with pain the doctor, without even thinking that much, will say, 'Why don't you give this new drug a try?' But we have been clamping down on prescription of non-generic drugs. We've created some specific protocols where we will only reimburse for non-generics in very narrow circumstances. We make sure that everyone knows this. And the doctors then are happy to comply. It saves a lot of money."*

EXAMPLE 2: PARTNERING WITH THE HUMAN RESOURCES DEPARTMENT

Let's say that you're a senior Human Resources executive who has had trouble getting the senior managers to see HR as anything other than a payroll function. And let's say that you want to give a presentation urging the senior leadership to proactively partner with HR to help achieve core business goals like growing revenue.

One of your three core points might be: "Each business unit will have its own internal HR staffer."

The natural questions that arise from that statement are "Why?" and "How will it work?"

So you would answer those questions.

"The reason that we're assigning each business unit an HR staffer is so that you will have an HR person who can become expert in your business unit's people needs. The HR staffer assigned to IT will learn exactly what kinds of people you will need to achieve your goals. The HR staffer assigned to sales will learn exactly what kinds of people you will need to achieve your sales goals. They will then be able to serve you better.

"So you may ask, 'How will it work?' Simple. They move in with you, attend your meetings, begin creating personnel analyses, succession plans, job descriptions, process documentation. They become expert in the people aspect of your business and helping you refine it."

Next, give evidence supporting your point.

"Let me give you an example. When I was at the Acme Bottling Company, I was the embedded HR specialist working with the marketing organization. I spent my first two months just shadowing the key executives. I was able to learn about the key personnel needs that they had. I was able to develop processes for backfilling the key positions. I was able to make sure that if we knew someone was going to be promoted out of a key position, we had another person properly trained to take over that key position. My deep understanding of the department's people needs played a key role in allowing the organization to achieve its goals."

KEY TAKEAWAY

The key to filling out your presentation is to keep each point simple. Ask yourself this: "What are the top two or three questions that the audience would ask about this point?" Answer those questions. Give an example or piece of data in support of your point. Then stop.

6

CLOSE BY RECAPPING YOUR THREE KEY POINTS

A Little Redundancy Builds Retention

Let's say that I come to you before your next presentation and offer you a "$300,000" challenge.

The challenge is that after the speech, I will approach three of your listeners and ask, "What were the presentation's three key points?" If each person can repeat back to me the three key messages, then you get the $300,000.

If that's the challenge, I promise that you will want to repeat those core messages enough times to ensure that the audience retains the message.

I believe this is a fundamental test of a presentation. If you can't get your listener to remember three key messages, then your message is a failure.

Getting the audience to retain key messages isn't hard. You just need to repeat the key messages throughout the presentation several times.

So here is how you recap. Once you've gone through the body of your presentation, remind your listeners of your three key messages. It could sound like this:

"There are three key messages here.

- *Managed care saves money for the state.*
- *Managed care improves the state's medical care.*
- *Managed care allows us to serve more people."*

Or how about:

"There are three key messages here.

- *Each department needs an HR specialist.*
- *Specialists conduct gap analyses identifying department needs.*
- *Specialists fill gaps in personnel needs."*

KEY TAKEAWAY

This isn't about eloquence. It's about being effective. Repeat the message to drive home your point. Collect $300,000.

7

END BY ASKING FOR SOMETHING

What Do You Want From Your Audience?

So many people want to be eloquent. But I have no idea how to teach eloquence. I don't think I can even define "eloquence."

But in the context of a presentation, I can define "effectiveness." It's answering all of your audience's questions so they can decide whether to move forward with your idea.

So what are the questions that listeners typically have at the end of a presentation?

There are typically two: "What do I do now?" and "What is the next step in the process?"

Once you've recapped your three key points, then you need to end by asking for something.

It typically should sound something like this:

"So what is the next step in the process? I recommend that we do a test of this approach with one of our divisions. If that works, I'd like to roll out the program across the organization."

Or this:

"So what do I want from you? I'd like you to approve my proposed budget of $500,000 for this project. I'll report back to you in three months with our progress."

KEY TAKEAWAY

If you want to be a leader, forget about eloquence. Instead, give clear direction. End your presentations by giving your audience a clear sense of what is next.

8

KEYS TO TELLING A GOOD STORY

Make Your Presentations Sing

Think of all the best presentations you've ever heard. They all have stories. If you want to be a good speaker, you need stories.

The formula for a good presentation story is as follows:

- Start with the point. You don't want people wondering why you're telling them a story.
- Tell the story chronologically. Anything else is too hard for your listeners to follow.
- Keep it tight, but give some details. The art of telling a story is finding the right balance between the number of details and the length of the story. Remember that you only have seven minutes total, so your story probably won't be longer than 30 to 60 seconds.

- The more personal the story the better. The best stories are personal to you.
- Remind the audience of the point at the end. Even if you told the point at the beginning, people forget. You need to remind them.

EXAMPLE OF A GOOD STORY

Let's go back to the story included in the presentation in Chapter 2. That presentation was given by a division president detailing his plan for reviving a manufacturing business that lost customers due to poor quality. One of his points is that the division can regain revenues simply by winning back customers who initially left in frustration.

He starts with the point: Customers will return if we fix the quality problems.

"The good news is that none of our customers wanted to leave us. We had served them well for years. And none have been happy with our competition. If we can convince them that we've fixed the quality problems, I'm confident they will return."

Then he tells a story chronologically, walking through what happened in the office of a lost client. He also includes some details. Notice that he doesn't say that he called on customers in general. He names the specific customer he called on. Those details add authenticity and make the story more persuasive.

> *"I know this because I've spent the last three months personally calling on our biggest accounts. Six weeks ago, I sat in the office of John Castro of Cantor Williams Jones. I went to see him with the intent of letting him vent, telling me why he left us. He said, 'I can't stand the solution we have right now. Our current supplier doesn't seem to be able to deliver on time. Ever. But it's a lesser of two evils thing. They're late, but your boxes were falling apart.'*

> *"When I asked him if he would give us another chance, he said he would consider placing a small order as a test. I then sent John Fredericks out to meet him and they've started to build a good relationship. I'm told that we're probably going to get that business back in six months. And I think we have similarly good stories with our other clients."*

Then he reminds the audience of the point at the end.

"The fact is that our clients loved us until we dropped the ball. They're willing to come back if we can show them we've made changes."

That story puts the listener in the office with an angry customer. It gives a feeling for the problem that the business is facing. Nothing is more persuasive than a well-told story.

KEY TAKEAWAY
Start with the point. Tell the story chronologically.
Keep it tight. The best stories are personal.
Remind the audience of the point at the end.

9

TRANSITIONS HELP YOUR LISTENERS

Keep Your Audience From Getting Lost

Good speakers always remember that listening is hard. It's hard to sit in the audience and capture information and process it. It's hard to try to keep all the points straight and figure out where all of it is going.

So the good speaker takes care to help the listener along the way. She makes certain that she puts up plenty of signposts to always keep the listener oriented. Those signposts say, "This is where we are! Don't be worried. You're not lost! All is well!"

Transitions are the signposts of your presentation. They keep the listener oriented.

To that end, you need a transitional statement at every turning point in your presentation. In the

"15 Minutes Including Q&A" approach, there are six transitions.

TRANSITION 1—FROM THE HOOK TO THE THREE POINT PREVIEW

"I'm going to talk about three things today. They are . . ."

TRANSITION 2—FROM THE THREE POINT PREVIEW TO POINT 1

"So let's talk about point 1, how we're going to save you money."

TRANSITION 3—FROM POINT 1 TO POINT 2

"So that's my first point. Now let's talk about my next major point, how we're going to save you time."

TRANSITION 4—FROM POINT 2 TO POINT 3

"So that's my second point. Now let's talk about the third point, how long it will take to implement the project."

TRANSITION 5—FROM POINT 3 TO THE RECAP

"So now, let's recap my three major points."

TRANSITION 6—FROM RECAP TO CLOSE

"So what is the next step?"

A lot of people worry that transitions aren't "smooth." But remember, the goal isn't to be smooth. The goal is to help the listener. So help them out with clean transitions.

KEY TAKEAWAY

Transitions are the signposts of your presentation. They keep the listener oriented. You need a transitional statement at every turning point in your presentation.

10

AN EVEN SIMPLER
PRESENTATION METHOD

Use Three Questions to Drive Your Message

What I've outlined so far is a simple way of creating a short, effective presentation. But there is an even easier approach that is highly effective, depending on the subject.

You start by introducing your topic. Then you say, "If I were you, I'd ask three questions about this topic." Write the questions on a flip chart. Answer the three questions. Then stop.

It's amazing how powerful this approach can be, especially when you're talking about complicated topics.

EXAMPLE 1

I was working with the head of supply chain operations for a large chain of gift shops. He was charged with explaining the complexities of his supply chain operation to several thousand store managers. And it was complicated. As he tried to explain all the complexities of operating a modern supply chain, he was getting frustrated. And the presentation was confusing.

"Do these store managers really care about how the supply chain functions?" I asked.

"Not really," he said.

"If these store managers could ask you three questions, what would they be?"

The supply chain manager had to think for only about a minute before he came up with three questions:

- How is supply chain operations working to improve our in-stock position?
- How can supply chain operations be more responsive to the stores?
- How is supply chain operations communicating changes to the stores more effectively?

Once he came up with those three questions, I said, "Why not just make that your presentation?"

That's what he did. His presentation went as follows:

"I'm here today to talk to you about what we're doing to improve the quality of our supply chain. Now I know that you don't really want to know everything there is to know about the supply chain. So I figured I'd focus on three questions that I think you'd like answers to about our supply chain."

He then laid out the three questions. Then he answered each question.

EXAMPLE 2

I was working with the new president of a healthcare products manufacturer. He had to give a speech in which he introduced himself to his sales force. He thought about laying out a complicated vision. I said, "What three questions do you think your sellers would want to know from their new president?" He came up with:

- Who are you?
- What is your goal for the business?
- What will you expect from the sales team?

He started his presentation by simply saying, "I know that I'm new to you. And my job today is to introduce myself to you and give you a feel for how I plan to run this organization. If I were you, I'd ask three questions." Then he laid out the questions. Then he proceeded to answer the questions. Then he stopped.

KEY TAKEAWAY

A quick and easy way to give a very effective presentation is to just pose the three questions that your audience would ask. Then answer those questions. Then stop.

11

CREATING SLIDES TO SUPPORT YOUR MESSAGE

Don't Let the Slides Overwhelm

Here is a conversation that takes place thousands of times a day across corporate America.

"Can you email me a copy of your presentation?"

"Sure. It's about 10 megabytes and 60 slides. It might take a while to come through."

Now I'm not against PowerPoint. But the fact that people think a deck of slides is synonymous with "your presentation" is a sign of how bad presentations have become. Preparing presentations has become an exercise in preparing slides. Instead, it should be an exercise in figuring out how to tell your story.

If you want to use slides well, you should only prepare your slides *after* you've figured out the "story" that you plan to tell your audience.

So let's say that you're a true believer in the "15 Minutes Including Q&A" approach. You would typically have six slides. Here is a presentation given by an attorney about how to avoid anti-trust liability. His hook focused on the business problem that he knew his listeners were concerned about: how to avoid anti-trust liability and possibly going to jail.

Hook

Stay Out of Jail and Avoid Fines

- Deal with competitors legally.
- Take care when harming a competitor.
- Watch your documents.

Three Point Preview

Deal with Competitors Legally

- Price
- Bid-volumes
- Strategic Plans
- Plans for Dealing with Competition

Point 1

Take Care When Harming a Competitor

- Tying
- Predatory Pricing
- Exclusivity Arrangements

Point 2

Watch Your Documents

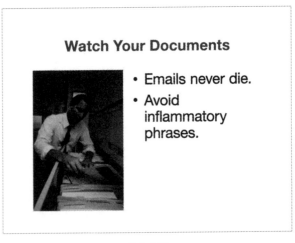

- Emails never die.
- Avoid inflammatory phrases.

Point 3

Stay Out of Jail and Avoid Fines

- Deal with competitors legally.
- Take care when harming a competitor.
- Watch your documents.

Recap

KEY TAKEAWAY

Don't create slides until you've figured out how you're going to lay out your overall story. Then figure out how to illustrate your message.

PART II

_____

ALLOW LISTENERS TO FILL IN THE BLANKS AND RAISE OBJECTIONS WITH Q&A

12

THE MAGIC OF Q&A

The Importance of Letting the Listeners Participate

If there is a secret sauce for the "15 Minutes Including Q&A" approach, it's Q&A. That's because Q&A is the element that fills in the gaps and gives a robust feel to your presentation.

I like to say that Q&A is "presentation duct tape." It fixes everything.

Lots of Q&A Fills in the Gaps in Your Presentation

Q&A allows the speaker to be focused on a few key messages and leave out the stuff that he judges to be less important. If the audience wants to hear about another issue, they can ask.

Let's say that you've decided that your message should focus on how a project will save money, save time, and increase job satisfaction. You might worry that you need to talk about how long the project will take. In your judgment, that's not an important issue. But others may disagree.

If you're a lousy presenter, you err on the side of inclusion. A voice in your head says to you, "Include a slide or two on how long the project will take. After all, someone might ask the question."

I'm saying that you should ignore that voice. Listening to that voice and including everything is how presentations start to smell. You start to include everything and your key messages get lost amid all the other stuff.

But leaving plenty of time for Q&A fixes this problem. You can feel comfortable in leaving things out. If your audience wants to know it, they can ask.

Lots of Q&A Fixes Persuasion Problems

In the world of sales, they say that customer objections are "selling opportunities." What that means is that when someone raises an objection, they're telling you, "I want to buy. But there is something that is in the way. If you can remove the objection, then I'll move closer to buying your idea."

The same is true with Q&A. If you're trying to sell an idea, you want your listeners to ask questions and raise objections. If you can remove those barriers, then you will be moving them closer to buying your idea.

Let's say that you're making the point that your project will increase overall job satisfaction for the employees involved. And let's say that there is a skeptic. If you've left time for Q&A, then that skeptic has time to raise his or her issues with your position. "You say that this project will increase overall job satisfaction, but how can you say that when we are going to have to lay off people as a result of this project?"

That's a great question. If you have a good answer, then you're going to move that skeptic closer to buying your idea. But you won't even get that question if you don't leave enough time for Q&A.

Q&A Improves Your Style

Most of us have a more engaged style during Q&A. I've seen it a million times. You stand up there to give a speech and you speak with all the personality of a house plant. Your voice is monotone. Your face is flat. Your eyes are fixed at the ground.

But then someone raises a hand and asks a question. Suddenly, your voice and face are animated. Why does this happen? "I'm always much more comfortable during Q&A," is what people say to me all the time.

We all feel more comfortable during Q&A because most of the time communication is a two-way street. The back-and-forth of Q&A is the norm. We use Q&A to speak in meetings, on the telephone, at lunch, in the car, etc. We feel more comfortable with Q&A because, for the most part, that is how we experience everyday conversation.

It's only when we stand up to give a speech that we break this back-and-forth pattern of communication. It throws most of us for a loop, and our style becomes stiff.

If Q&A is more comfortable for us, then why not include more of it?

KEY TAKEAWAY

Make Q&A a major part of your presentation strategy. Q&A allows the audience to guide the message, filling in missing information. It also gives the speaker the chance to persuade by responding to objections. And finally, it improves your communication style.

13

PREPARING FOR Q&A

Don't Get Stumped by Questions

I was working with a CPA once who told me that he hated taking questions during presentations. He would always put questions off to the end and hoped that no one would ask any.

When I asked why, he said, "I never know what people will ask and I don't like to be caught unprepared."

Of course, that is a problem. If you don't like getting questions, the "15 Minutes Including Q&A" approach is not going to be a good fit for you.

But there is no reason why you should be unprepared for questions. It's simply a matter of taking the time to prepare.

Henry Kissinger, the former Secretary of State, once said to a gathering of news reporters, "Does anyone have any questions for the answers I've prepared?"

The best speakers spend a great deal of time trying to determine what questions they will get. You should do the same. We recommend writing down 10 to 15 possible questions and then coming up with answers.

Do that and you won't dread questions. You'll look forward to them.

KEY TAKEAWAY

You're not ready for your presentation unless you've prepared for Q&A. Write down all possible questions and practice delivering the answers.

14

GOODS ANSWERS ARE TIGHT

If They Want to Know How to Build a Watch, They'll Ask

When we coach executives to speak to Wall Street, the investor relations departments usually do a wonderful job of putting together "briefing books" that give detailed answers to every question that an investment analyst might ask.

The only problem is that you don't get to read your answers from the briefing books. Rather, you have to give spoken answers.

So to prepare the executives for the questions, we make the executives do "one sentence" drills. That is, we make them give one-sentence answers to the questions. The idea is to help the executive develop a habit of giving tight answers.

Tight answers are far superior to longer answers.

First, tight answers are more persuasive. If you answer quickly, your confidence instills confidence in the listener. They think, "Wow. She seemed to know the answer. She must be right." By contrast, if you give a long, winding answer, the listener could think, "It sounds like she's working this out as she's speaking. That doesn't inspire confidence."

Second, tight answers don't overwhelm the listener. Tight answers give the listener what they want, quickly. If someone asks you the time, they don't usually want to know how to build the entire watch. And if they do want to know how to build the watch, they can ask.

Note that I don't think you should only give one-sentence answers. But you should start with the simple answer and then explain. Then stop.

EXAMPLE 1

"How long will the project take?"

Bad answer: *"Well, we need to have a couple of meetings with people in the field first. During those meetings, we're going to gather a lot of data about preferences. Sometimes their pref-*

erences can dictate a lot of extra work on our part. However, if their preferences are pretty straightforward, we probably won't have to do much in terms of follow-up. If that's the case, then we estimate that the project will take between three and six months."

Good answer: *"We estimate it will take no more than six months. The key will be whether we can get the key data from field personnel quickly."*

EXAMPLE 2

"How much will the project cost?"

Bad answer: *"Well, right now we don't have costs for steel. The most important cost on this job will be the steel. That's what we're going to use to erect the core of the building and that is what drives much of our costs. So assuming that we can get those costs within the first week, we'll know. My initial estimate will be $20 million."*

Good answer: *"Our estimate is $20 million. The key issue is whether we can get the steel at* *the cost we expect. We'll know that within the first week of the project."*

KEY TAKEAWAY

Start with a tight one- or two-sentence
answer. Give a little explanation. Stop.

15

TAKE QUESTIONS AT ANY TIME

Audience Questions are Too Important to Delay

When I was practicing law, I attended a training session where the facilitator didn't like taking questions out of order. If you asked a question that he was going to cover later, he would say, "Let's put that question in the parking lot."

And then he would write the question in a corner of the whiteboard that he had lined to look like a little parking lot. He had actually drawn little "parking spaces" for the questions.

It was stupid and humiliating. I didn't want my question in the parking lot. I wanted my question answered, thank you very much.

And that's the bottom line: When someone asks a question, answer it immediately.

You're There for the Listeners

Look, you may want to answer the question later. You may have set up your presentation to flow a special way. But if your listener asks a question, something's bothering her. There's something that she wants to know or doesn't understand. She doesn't care about the "special flow" that you've put together. All she wants is a little help. And since the presentation is 100 percent for your listeners' benefit, you need to stop and answer the question.

Taking Questions Leads to More Questions—And That's Good

If you answer questions throughout your presentation, listeners will interrupt you more and ask more questions. And that's great! You want people interrupting, questioning, probing, and "kicking the tires" of your presentation. The best presentations are conversations where the listeners participate and get what they want. If there are lots of questions, then the chances are that your listeners are going to go away with what they need.

Getting Back on Track is Easy

The main reason that people don't like to take questions out of order is that they're afraid that their precious "flow" is going to get thrown off.

Not to worry. Here is how you keep your flow.

If the question is something you're going to address later, here's what you say: "Well, I'm going to talk more about that later. But let me give you a quick answer . . ."

If they ask a question that takes you a little off track, answer the question fully and then say, "And that leads me back to the second point I was going to make, how we plan to save the company $1 million next year."

Don't worry about whether it actually "leads you back." It's just a tool to help you control the conversation.

KEY TAKEAWAY

You're speaking for the benefit of the audience.
If someone has a question, stop and answer it.

16

HOW TO GET LOTS OF QUESTIONS

Create an Environment Where Q&A is Welcome

One of the biggest concerns people have with devoting half the time to Q&A is a fear that no one will ask questions.

But that won't happen if you create a Q&A-friendly environment. There are several things you can do to loosen up the audience and make them feel free to jump in and ask questions.

Tell the Audience What You Expect

The first step in creating a Q&A-friendly environment is to explain the format. Say something like, "I have 15 minutes with you. I'm going to leave half of that time for Q&A. So please jump in and ask questions at any time. I want you to jump in, probe, push back, etc."

This simple statement lets the audience know that they're expected to participate. It also lets them know that this is not going to be one of those overstuffed presentations where there really isn't time for Q&A.

Repeatedly Pause for the Questions

After each of your three points, pause and ask, "What questions do you have about this?" Then you need to pause. Really pause. Pause for five to ten seconds. It will seem like an eternity to you. But if you wait, people will get the idea that you really want them to ask questions.

If they don't ask anything during the first pause, they usually will during the second pause.

Plant Questions

If you're really worried that no one will ask questions, then put a plant in the audience. Simply ask a friend who will be attending the presentation to raise questions. Usually you just need one person to break the ice to get the questions flowing.

Ask the Audience Questions

During my workshops, when I come to a place where people often question one of my ideas, I'll raise the question myself. "It's at this point in my presentation where people sometimes argue with me," I say. "What is the counterargument here?"

Show Your Delight When Someone Asks Questions

You don't have to say "Great question!" I find that condescending. But you can simply take every question enthusiastically, smiling and showing your delight that the audience is participating. If you make them feel good for asking questions, they'll want to ask more.

KEY TAKEAWAY
To get lots of questions during a
presentation, create a Q&A-friendly
environment. Make the audience feel how
important it is for them to participate.

PART III

DELIVER THE PRESENTATION WITH INTENSITY

17

YOUR AUTHENTIC SPEAKING STYLE

Connect While Still Being Yourself

Imagine that you're at dinner with a close friend or family member. And you're talking with a great deal of intensity about something that you're passionate about.

That is the kind of presentation style we recommend. We want you to speak with the same intensity that you bring when you're talking to a close friend about a subject you feel passionate about.

Of course the problem when you're speaking in a business setting is that you're not speaking with close personal friends. It's not a dinner conversation. It's a business presentation. And you're not the same person in business as you are with your friends.

So how do you get back to that "personal style" when you're giving a business presentation?

Make Great Eye Contact and Exaggerate

First comes eye contact. No one can be a good presenter if they're not making good eye contact with the audience. Eye contact is the point where actual contact with the audience takes place. It's the point of connection. And without connection, you're lost.

Next comes exaggeration. You need to exaggerate your facial energy, your gestures, and your voice energy. Why exaggerate? Because when we're speaking in a business setting, we pull in. We become a more conservative version of ourselves. We become flat. Indeed, the number one issue with business presenters is that they speak with too little energy.

"But I don't want to come across like a television huckster!" That's the pushback we get when we urge people to exaggerate their energy. The huckster issue is not a problem because of the "authenticity paradox."

The Authenticity Paradox

When we exaggerate, over-energizing our facial energy, vocal energy, and gestures, we don't come across as "over the top." We just get back to the personal style that we have when we're with friends and we're intense.

I like to call this the "authenticity paradox." I want you to be authentic. But when you're standing in a conference room, you don't feel authentic. So to find that authenticity, exaggerate your energy. In a sense, you need to act like an exaggerated version of yourself to get back to an authentic version of yourself.

KEY TAKEAWAY

To connect with an audience, you need to make great eye contact and speak with the same intensity that you bring to an animated dinner conversation.

18

GREAT STYLE STARTS WITH EYE CONTACT

The Key to Connection With an Audience

Sometimes I feel like telling people that they should physically grab their prospects by the shirt and say, "Pay attention to my presentation! I want you to understand these ideas because they can help your business succeed. So listen!"

Of course, you can't do that, and I would never suggest such a thing. That's why eye contact is so important. The closest you can come to physically grabbing someone and saying, "Pay attention!" is making strong eye contact. Indeed, great eye contact is the most intimate thing you can do during a presentation to help connect you with your listeners.

While most people in business do okay with eye contact, they don't maximize their connection with the audience by holding eye contact long enough. Most business people just look out at their audience and graze them with their eyes, never really connecting with anyone longer than a fleeting moment.

The idea is to make eye contact long enough for the person to feel as if you've connected with them, and to give you some sign that you've connected. Maybe it's a nod. Maybe it's a smile. Maybe they stick out their tongue at you. You just want to connect.

Have Miniature Conversations with Individuals

Great eye contact happens when you look at individual members of the audience long enough to feel like they are responding you. As I write this section of this book, I'm on a flight from Chicago after delivering a presentation skills program to a group of prominent architects.

In demonstrating the type of eye contact that was necessary, I looked around the room and connected with Ingrid, an interior designer from Frankfurt, Germany. As I spoke, I maintained the eye contact long enough until I saw her beginning to smile. "Now, I've got you," I thought. "I'll move to someone else now."

We do an eye contact exercise in our workshops that illustrates powerfully how important—and often difficult—it is to make appropriate eye contact with members of your audience. We have one of our participants stand in front of the group. Then we ask all members of the group to raise a hand.

"Talk about what you did on your summer vacation," we tell the participant. "As you look at each person, you need to make eye contact long enough to get them to put down their hand. And they won't put their hand down *unless they feel the connection*. If you just graze past their eyes without really holding their attention, they are going to leave their hands up. You need to hold the eye contact *through a thought*."

It's an interesting exercise because many of the participants find it very difficult to get those hands to go down. Sure, they make eye contact, most people do, but they don't hold it long enough. Usually, they make the eye contact quickly and move to the next person, but then they realize that the person they just left still has her hand up in the air. For most people, to get the hands down, you really have to hold eye contact longer than they are used to or comfortable with.

That's the point. What you think is comfortable in terms of eye contact is probably not enough to give your listener a sense of connection.

A good rule of thumb is to hold the eye contact *three to five seconds* before moving on. For those who aren't used to it, this will seem like a long time. Perhaps it will feel inappropriately long, but it won't bother your listeners. To the contrary, they'll just get the very nice sense that you're connecting with them in a personal way.

KEY TAKEAWAY
To make great eye contact, work your way around the room by having random miniature conversations with individuals.

19

FACIAL ENERGY THAT CONNECTS

Show Intensity With the Face

A key way to improve your ability to connect with audiences is to improve your facial energy.

Why? Because people are watching your facial expressions and making judgments about you based on them.

In a study in Great Britain, scientists took routine objects and held them in front of infants' faces. At the same time, the scientists measured the babies' brain waves to indicate how interesting the baby found the object. For example, they would hold a cup in front of a baby and measure the brain waves. Then they would do the same thing with a pen, a book, a fork, etc. Finally, they would put a photograph of a human face in front of the baby. The face made the brain waves run off the charts.

I tell you about this study because it shows just how attuned we are to the face. Even as infants, we are fascinated with the face.

We have an enormous ability to be visually expressive with our face. Social scientist Paul Ekman has determined that we can make 3,000 meaningful facial expressions.

Yet in business, most of us rely on only one expression, the bland "business face." As a result, most of us look flat when we're speaking.

Exaggerate Your Facial Energy

What do we recommend?

Once again, we recommend exaggeration. During our workshops, we routinely urge our clients to exaggerate their facial energy. "Smile too much!" we say. "Exaggerate your facial expression!" "Overdo it with the face!"

Of course, the pushback we get is always the same. "That feels strange. It doesn't feel natural."

And of course they're right. It does *feel* odd, especially if you're not used to it.

But the goal when you're learning to be a good speaker isn't necessarily to feel comfortable. Few things about public speaking feel natural when you first do them. How you feel isn't the relevant issue. The relevant issue is how you look.

The best way to improve your facial energy is to give your presentation while looking in a mirror. As you speak, try stuff. Try smiling too much. Try doing too much with your eyebrows. Try speaking like you're angry. Try speaking like you're frustrated.

The mirror gives you instant feedback and you get an instant feeling about what works and what doesn't.

KEY TAKEAWAY
Your facial energy can communicate a great deal to your audience. Take your face out of park.

20

GESTURES THAT HELP YOU CONNECT

Your Arms And Hands Can Add Energy

When it comes to gestures, you can read a million little pieces of advice. Make big gestures. Clasp your hands in front. No, be sure that you hold them at your sides. Keep your elbows up. Don't point. Don't gesture with your thumbs.

Here's our primary bit of gesture advice: **The gesture bone is connected to the voice bone.**

It may sound silly. But it's true. What I'm saying is that the energy you show with your hands, your arms, and your body is usually reflected in your face, your voice, and your eyes.

With that in mind, gesture more. Move your hands around. Get your arms up. Move your body. Work up a sweat! The more you move your body, the more energetic you will be generally.

I've seen it a million times. We had an accountant in a workshop. And he was coming across as incredibly flat. "But I'm an accountant," he said, as if that were a good excuse.

The next time he stood to give a presentation, I gave him the following instruction. "I want you to get your arms moving. Over-gesture. Work up a sweat."

He did what I asked, and a funny thing happened. As he gestured more, he became more energized in general. His face, voice, and eyes relaxed and he started speaking with the kind of animated tone you associate with an animated argument over dinner.

That's the point.

Use your body to energize your face, voice, and eyes.

KEY TAKEAWAY
Don't be afraid of intense gestures.
They add energy.

21

VOICE ENERGY

Passion Sells

The voice is an incredibly important tool for selling an idea. The passion in the voice sells.

To see this, you have to look no further than television hucksters like Vince the ShamWow guy and Billy Mays. These guys know that if they sound excited, it will get the audience excited.

When I use this example, people get nervous. "I don't want to sound like a television pitchman or a used car salesman!" And I don't want that for you either.

But think of vocal energy as a continuum of 1 to 100. If you speak with no energy at all, that's a one on the energy scale. If you speak like Billy Mays, the late television pitchman, that's a 100 on the energy scale. Most people in business have vocal energy in the 10-20 range. That's too flat.

You don't have to go all the way to 100 or have a style like Billy Mays. But couldn't you get to 50 or 60?

Exaggerate Your Voice Energy

So what do you do?

Once again, you need to learn to exaggerate. We tell people to "overdo it." Give me way too much excitement, passion, and intensity in that voice. When your voice gets soft, make it too soft. When your voice gets loud, make it too loud. When you pause, pause too long. And when you speak quickly, speak too quickly.

I know that it's going to feel strange. It's going to feel like you're overdoing it. "That feels like I'm a used car salesman." But it won't sound that way. If you think you're overdoing it, it will probably sound good to the audience.

A Simple Voice Energy Exercise

In our workshops, we combat monotone voices with a classic voice coaching/acting exercise. The idea is to eliminate the monotone by putting action in the voice. We urge participants to read a simple script which forces them to vary speed and volume.

Please read these aloud as suggested:

- **Read loudly:** "Volume adds emphasis to an important word or phrase."
- **Read softly:** "A whisper acts as a magnet and draws the audience to you."
- **Read fast:** "Speaking rapidly excites and energizes the audience."
- **Read slowly:** "A slow rate of speech creates a mood of awe and wonder."
- **Read with pauses:** "A pause shows poise . . . control . . . confidence . . . use it . . . master it."

It's amazing how difficult this exercise is for some people. For example, someone will read the first two parts of the exercise. They know they're supposed to read loudly and then get down to a whisper. But they won't be able to do it. They will read each sentence with the exact same volume. I'll turn to the person sitting next to the participant who just read and say, "How did she do?"

"No variation at all."

The reader will look stunned. She is completely convinced that her voice was loud and then soft.

"Did it feel like you were getting loud and soft?" I'll say.

"Yes."

Yet everyone in the class will agree that her voice didn't change at all. I've seen this happen enough times to know that the person really did believe that her voice was getting louder and softer. In her head, I'm certain her voice is changing volume.

The problem is that this person, like most of us, doesn't really know how she sounds to the outside world. Most of us have listened to our own voices on a tape recorder only to recoil, saying, "I don't really sound like that!" But we do. We just don't have a true sense of how we really sound.

It's important to work on varying your voice to learn to control how you sound.

KEY TAKEAWAY
The passion in your voice sells ideas.
Show intensity by making your voice go
up and down like a roller coaster.

22

THE VALUE OF A VIDEO CAMERA

See How Others See You

One of the best ways to improve your speaking style is to watch a video of yourself giving a presentation.

Why is video so valuable? Because for most people, how you think you come across is much different than how you actually come across. I see it every time I work with someone.

"This time," I say, "I'd like for you to really exaggerate everything. Exaggerate your facial energy. Exaggerate your vocal variety. Gesture way too much. Do too much with your eyebrows. Just overdo it."

The client will look at me like I'm nuts. But then they'll do their best.

"So how did that feel?" I'll ask.

"It felt like I was a used car salesman."

"Remember that you said that," I'll say. Then we will replay the video.

"What do you think?" I ask. "Does it look over the top?"

The client will look at the tape and shake her head. "No," she'll admit. "It actually looks good." One way for most of us to learn to control how we look is to see how we look on video.

KEY TAKEAWAY
To really improve, you need to see how
you come across to others. Use video
to see how you come across.

23

THE VALUE OF REHEARSAL

The Key to Greatness

I received this question once from a magazine writer who was doing a story about how to be a better speaker: "If you could give me only one sentence on how to be a great speaker, what would it be?"

"I don't need an entire sentence," I said. "I only need one word. 'Rehearse.'"

The fact is that rehearsal by itself can make you a substantially better speaker. You need to rehearse your presentation and how you're going to answer the questions.

Out loud! Like it's a play!

Presenting is a spoken art. You can't prepare by flipping through your slides saying, "I know what I'm going to say here. I know what I'm going to say here. I know what . . ."

To be good you need to rehearse out loud. We don't want you to write out your speech word for word. And we don't want you to memorize it. Just make a few notes and begin vocalizing your message.

Rehearsal Helps You Figure Out How to Say It Smoothly

By rehearsing out loud, you'll get a feel for what sounds right. You can't do that by just flipping through your slides.

Let's say that you're going to talk about how your plan for building a hospital resembles another project you did last year. How are you going to articulate that thought?

The first time you try to say it, you might start out like this:

> *"Last year we built a hospital with 15 floors and a cardiac wing in Denver, Colorado. They were very worried about patient safety because the last time they had work done, one of their patients tripped over a stray piece of a drywall."*

Does that say it the way you want? Maybe.

However, it might sound better if you said it like this:

"We understand that you're concerned about safety. We heard about how on a previous project one of your nurses slipped on some paint and sprained her wrist. We actually had another client just like you in Denver. On a previous job, a patient had tripped over some drywall."

I'm not suggesting that one way is right and one is wrong. All I'm saying is that you need to figure out the best way to say the thing—to get the words to come out of your mouth. And you can't do that without rehearsal.

By practicing, you can find all the dead ends where you don't want to go. You can hear how it sounds and say, "That doesn't sound right. I'd better try that again."

You need to rehearse over and over again so that when you get up there to deliver your presentation, you sound smooth and confident.

KEY TAKEAWAY

Rehearse out loud from beginning to end like it's a play. Then do it again and again until you're ready.

24

OVERCOMING NERVES, PART I

Rehearsal Beats Stage Fright

It's no wonder public speaking is considered everyone's number one fear, beating out death and spiders. Standing up and speaking feels extremely unnatural for most people. Most of us feel that the most natural way to speak is one-on-one, having a conversation over a conference table, or in a more intimate setting. So standing up to speak takes us out of that comfort zone and makes us feel judged.

I've heard many cures for stage fright. Picture your audience naked. Take drugs. Do push-ups. Use mental imagery. All of these ideas probably work to some extent. But in my experience, public speaking anxiety is something that doesn't lend itself to easy fixes.

The most important thing you can do to deal with stage fright is rehearse. You need to practice your presentation over and over again out loud. You need to develop something akin to vocal muscle memory. When the nerves kick in, you'll rely on that muscle memory to get you through it.

Try practicing with the television on. The television serves as a distraction just as nerves are a distraction. If you can deliver your presentation with the television playing, you should be able to shut out the nerves and get through your presentation.

KEY TAKEAWAY
To overcome anxiety, practice a lot.

25

OVERCOMING NERVES, PART II

Memorize Your First Two Lines

To overcome anxiety, practice the first two sentences so much that you could say them if a bomb went off.

You're most nervous when you first stand up. If you nail the beginning, you're going to relax a little. Your preparation will kick in. The words will start to flow.

On the other hand, if you're nervous and you flub the beginning, you're going to tighten up. The rest of the presentation will be difficult.

I once had to give a presentation to a large Rotary Club. I was particularly nervous. But I knew my first line cold. It was, "There was a study done of the way we communicate. It studied the different impressions we make when we speak." I must have said that line 50 times in my head as I waited for my time to speak.

When I stood to speak, I nailed those two lines and relaxed. Everything flowed well from there.

KEY TAKEAWAY

Knowing the first two lines cold helps you relax by getting you off to a good start at the beginning of your presentation.

CONCLUSION

PRACTICE THE GOLDEN RULE OF PRESENTING

Ultimately, the "15 Minutes Including Q&A" approach is about practicing what I call the Golden Rule of Presenting:

Present unto others as you would have them present unto you.

Do you like listening to long presentations? Of course not. So keep the presentation to no more than seven minutes.

Do you like listening to presentations that are overloaded with too many points? Me either. So keep it to just three key messages.

Do you like it when people clearly transition between points? Of course you do. So make sure that you always tell your listeners when you're moving to another big idea.

Do you like it when people tell stories? Yes. Then be sure that you use stories.

Do you like having the opportunity to ask lots of questions? Probably. So be sure that you leave your audience the chance to ask lots of questions.

Do you like it when you get long rambling answers to your questions? Of course not. So be sure that you keep your answers tight.

Do you like listening to speakers that sound bored? Of course not. So be sure that you speak with energy.

Do you like listening to speakers who have to constantly rely on their notes and don't seem prepared? Of course not. So rehearse your presentations.

From now on, limit your presentations to 15 minutes including Q&A. Your audiences will thank you.

ABOUT THE AUTHOR

Joey Asher is president of Speechworks, a communication and selling skills coaching firm that helps professionals and executives learn how to create and deliver great presentations.

He has worked with clients in a wide variety of industries including financial services, manufacturing, retail, consulting, accounting, real estate, architecture, financial services, insurance, high tech, cable, and law.

Joey's background is both as an attorney and as a newspaper reporter. In addition to running Speechworks, he is an instructor at the Georgia Tech College of Management. He has worked as an adjunct professor of law at Emory University School of law and was an attorney at Troutman Sanders in Atlanta. Prior to law school, he worked as a newspaper reporter for the Gannett newspaper chain in Georgia and New York. Joey graduated from Cornell University and Emory University Law School.

Joey lives in Atlanta with his wife Johanna and children Benjamin, Elliott, and Annie.

ABOUT SPEECHWORKS

Speechworks has been helping clients create and deliver winning presentations since 1986. Offerings include small, on-camera workshops, seminars for larger groups, and one-on-one executive coaching. Speechworks coaches also consult on specific presentations and help teams prepare for important new business presentations. To learn more about Speechworks go to www.speechworks.net or call 404-266-0888.